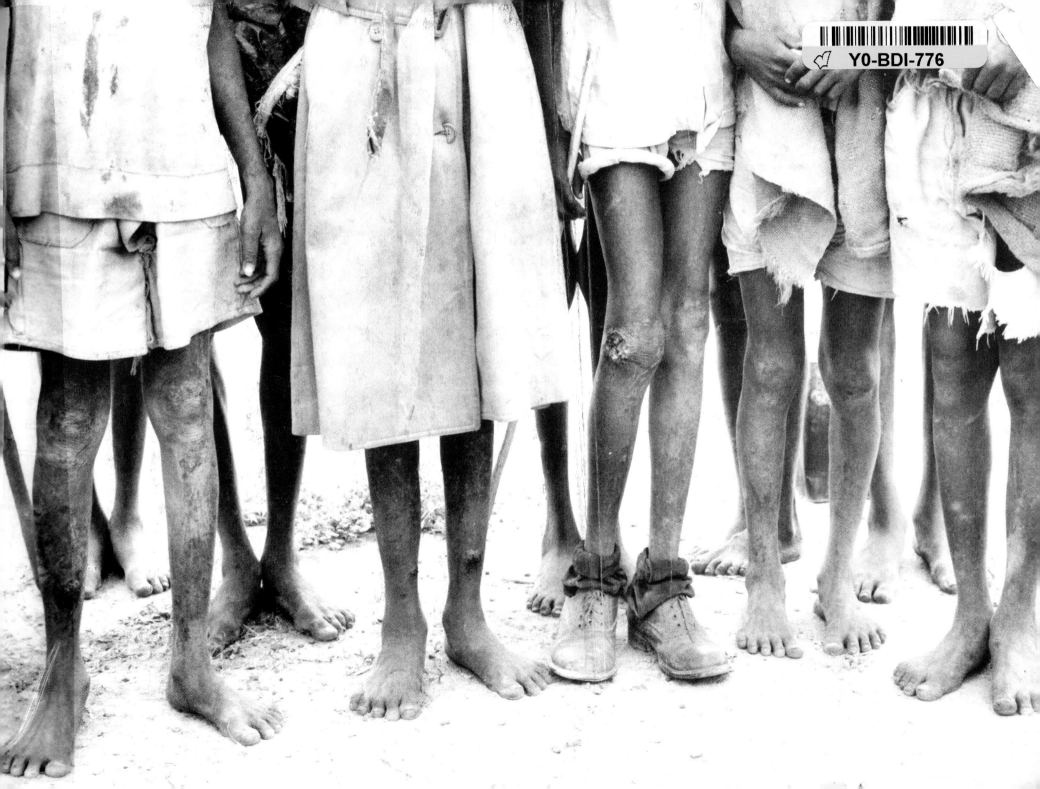

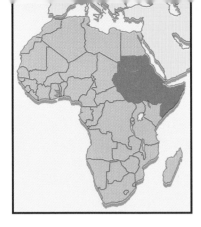

Refugee children tell
their stories in words
and paintings

One day we had to run!

Sybella Wilkes

The Millbrook Press
Brookfield, Connecticut

Contents

The terms "refugee" and "displaced person" are both used in this book. These definitions may help you:

What is a refugee?
A refugee is someone who has fled across a national border from his or her home country, or is unable to return to it, because of a well-founded fear that he or she will be persecuted for reasons of race, religion, nationality or political opinion. Refugees who cross borders because of famine are not necessarily covered by international protection, unlike refugees fleeing from war and so on.

What is a displaced person?
A displaced person is someone who has been forced to move to another part of his or her own country because of war, famine, or disaster.

◄ **Opposite:** painting by Liban Ahmed Habib, aged 10 years, Ethiopian, Ifo refugee camp. "The Somali old men are all waiting outside the school saying, 'Paint this, say this, don't say this, don't paint this.' I think it is very funny."

First published in Great Britain by
Evans Brothers Limited
2A Portman Mansions; Chiltern Street
London W1M 1LE

Published in the United States by
The Millbrook Press
2 Old New Milford Road
Brookfield, Connecticut 06804

© in the maps Evans Brothers Limited 1994
© in the text, photographs and children's paintings
Sybella Wilkes 1994

Printed and bound in Barcelona, Spain by Cronion, S.A.

Project editor: Su Swallow
Design, maps & page make-up: TJ Graphics

The photographs and paintings in this book are the property of the UNHCR. All the photographs are reproduced with the permission of **Panos Moumtzis** with the exception of the following: **Fiona McDougall** p 9, 47 & 58 (top right), cover (front left); **J. Mohr** p 37 (right); **Betty Press** p 17, 25 (middle left); 30 & 50; **Wendy Stone** endpapers, p 16 & 51 (left). The author wishes to thank: Sironka Averdung, Care International, Jacaranda Designs, Louisa Lockwood, Nina Joachim Trust (Durham University, UK), Radda Barnen, Alabel Derib, John Mungai, Stephen, Refugee Council, Jill Rutter, Save the Children Fund, UNHCR, Ian Lethbridge, Panos Moumtzis, Millicent Mutuli, Lois Williams and, of course, **all the refugee children who told their stories and painted their pictures for this book.**

Library of Congress Cataloging-in-Publication Data
Wilkes, Sybella.
One day we had to run! : refugee children tell their stories in words and paintings / by Sybella Wilkes.
p. cm.
Includes bibliographical references and index.
ISBN 1-56294-557-2 lib.bdg.
1-56294-844-X pbk.
1-56294-584-X tr.
1. Refugee children--Kenya--Juvenile literature.
(1. Refugees--Kenya. 2. Children's writings.
3. Children's art.) I. Title.
HV640.4.K4W55 1994
362.87'083--dc20   94-3743 CIP AC

Foreword

This book communicates in a direct and vivid way the intensely personal experience of a group of young refugees in the Horn of Africa. Through their eyes we relive the drama of their flight and the events that led up to it. We feel the fear and bewilderment they have suffered — and we wonder at their stubborn faith that the future is yet a hopeful place. We have much to learn from the words and pictures of these young people and from their courage in relating what has happened to them and to their families.

The stories these children tell us are not unique to people forced to flee their homes in one corner of one continent. All over the world, children are falling victim to disaster — both natural and man made. With alarming frequency, violence, upheaval, and war are taking their toll, permanently scarring young lives. Today in Rwanda, Bosnia-Hercegovina, and even in our own inner cities, conflicts created and carried out by adults are traumatizing, even killing, our young people.

Upholding the rights of children everywhere to special care and protection is a cornerstone of Save the Children's worldwide work. It was Save the Children's founder, Britishwoman Eglantyne Jebb, who wrote the world's first charter on children's rights, a work adopted in 1924 by the League of Nations. Later, in 1990, this charter was incorporated into the United Nations convention on the Rights of the Child, an international treaty ratified by more than 150 nations.

The International Save the Children Alliance has remained at the forefront of efforts to improve the standard of quality of care for refugees and displaced children and adults. This confederation, made up of 24 independent Save the Children organizations that work in more than 100 countries, has become a proponent of programs addressing the long-term psycho-social needs of refugee and displaced children. Building on its groundbreaking work in rehabilitating child soldiers in Mozambique, Save the

Children of the United States is taking the lead in worldwide efforts to help war-affected children and youths use art, dance, and theater to work through their trauma and successfully rejoin their families and communities. The works collected by Sybella Wilkes and presented in this book represent a similar effort.

Charles MacCormack
President
Save the Children
United States

Children's words; children's brushstrokes

The stories and pictures in this book are written and painted by refugee children in Kenya. They were done so that children in other parts of the world could understand what it is like to be a refugee. The stories are the children's own words; the pictures the children's own brushstrokes.

It is very difficult for these children to deal with the emotional horrors they have experienced. The idea that "a problem shared is a problem halved" does not really apply to children. Many find it hard to put how they feel into words, and are reluctant to discuss their experiences. I found the Sudanese children particularly difficult to talk to. Robbed of their childhood innocence by the civil war, they were scared to talk in case they said anything that their elders disapproved of. They often repeated well-rehearsed phrases about the "condition of Sudan" which told me nothing about their own feelings and experiences. Many of the children found my questions stupid and obvious. Yes, of course they had seen dead and dying people; so what? But when asked, "How do you feel about this?" they would withdraw into themselves and refuse to reply.

However, it was the children who helped me to find a way of communicating. Having spent several awkward hours with a group of Somali children who were telling me how they had reached Kenya, one of them said to me, "Why are you asking so many questions?" When I replied that I wanted to tell their stories to other children in the world, they brightened up enormously.

"Do you think they would like to hear the story about the lion that was larger than a camel and faster than a horse?" asked one of them.

Children who had previously been bored and shy came to life. I realized that if we had fun together I would learn more about them and they would learn to relax. Wherever I went after that I carried an armful of comics and story books. I

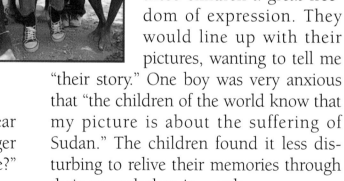

would tell them the stories that I had heard as a child and, in return, they would tell me their own stories and fairytales.

I worked with a Kenyan artist, Sironka Averdung, to teach the children how to use paints. Painting gave these children a great freedom of expression. They would line up with their pictures, wanting to tell me "their story." One boy was very anxious that "the children of the world know that my picture is about the suffering of Sudan." The children found it less disturbing to relive their memories through their artwork than in words.

Where do refugee children come from?

Why do these countries suffer from famine?

Famine in the Horn of Africa (see map, p. 11) has brought much attention to this region. Pictures of suffering have appeared on television screens and in newspapers all over the world. Many people now connect the countries of Somalia, Sudan, and Ethiopia with war and famine. But why do war and famine go together in these countries?

Many people live a hand-to-mouth existence in the Horn of Africa. They depend entirely upon the crops they grow and the animals they keep for food. When their lives are disrupted by war they are often forced to abandon their precious crops and animals. Famine and disease can easily become greater threats to the population of a country at war than the fighting itself. Many of the children of Somalia, Sudan, and Ethiopia will die, not directly as a result of the war itself, but from a lack of food.

Refugee children are children without a country or a home. Sometimes they no longer even have a family. They are children without a childhood.

As these children flee conflict, hatred and persecution, they see terrible suffering. Sometimes they are abandoned in the panic to escape, or are forced to take sides in wars they do not understand. Already shattered by the loss of their homes, possessions, and often their entire way of life, the long journey to safety can be even more traumatic for refugee children. They may face danger, exhaustion, and misery every step of the way. Many refugee children know what it is like to be hungry, day after day.

Refugees: a worldwide crisis

Over the last 40 years, the numbers of refugees have increased dramatically. When the United Nations High Commissioner for Refugees (UNHCR) was set up in 1951 there were one million refugees in the world. Today, there are about 19 million refugees. This reflects the growing instability in the world today. It is frightening to think that during the last four decades, 19 times more people have been forced to flee their homes as a result of war, persecution, and famine.

Every day, somewhere in the world, children become refugees. Of the 19 million refugees in the world, over half are children. They flee their countries because their lives are in danger. This book records the dreams, the nightmares, the stories, and the fairy tales of refugee children. It also tries to explain some of the reasons why these children are refugees.

Refugees in Africa

There are about six million refugees in Africa, the largest number of refugees in one continent in the world. This book concentrates on the lives of refugee children in the Horn of Africa — the northeastern region of Africa that juts out between the Red Sea and the Indian Ocean. During the past 30 years the Horn of Africa has experienced a

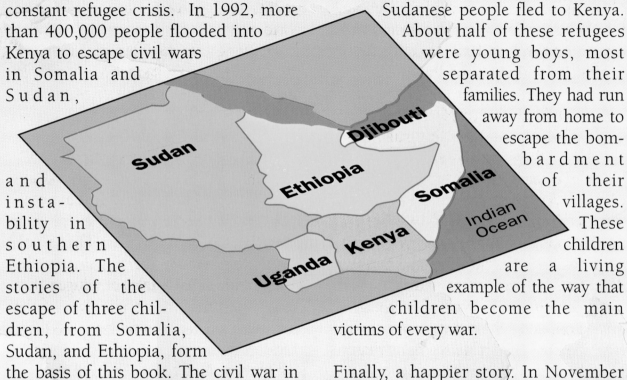

constant refugee crisis. In 1992, more than 400,000 people flooded into Kenya to escape civil wars in Somalia and Sudan, and instability in southern Ethiopia. The stories of the escape of three children, from Somalia, Sudan, and Ethiopia, form the basis of this book. The civil war in Somalia is being fought between rival clans battling for power and territory. As a result of this civil war, 10 percent of the Somali population lives outside the country's borders.

Meanwhile, the fighting in the civil war in southern Sudan became so fierce that, in May 1992, 20,000 Sudanese people fled to Kenya. About half of these refugees were young boys, most separated from their families. They had run away from home to escape the bombardment of their villages. These children are a living example of the way that children become the main victims of every war.

Finally, a happier story. In November 1992, 40,000 Ethiopian refugees in camps at Walda and Banissa in Kenya began to return home. Because of an agreement between the various clans of the Oromo in Ethiopia, the refugees at last felt safe to go back to their own country.

Chronology

1956 Sudan gains independence. By 1958, civil war is raging between the north and south, and southern Sudanese flee to neighboring countries.

1972 Agreement made between the government of Sudan and the tribes in the south. Hundreds of thousands of southern Sudanese refugees return to Sudan.

1978 Somalis living in Ethiopia flee to neighboring regions as the war between Somalia and Ethiopia rages over the Ogaden region of Ethiopia. Over 500,000 people are forced to flee.

1983 People leave southern Sudan as the civil war between the north and the south begins again. By 1990 an estimated 400,000 refugees have escaped to Ethiopia, as well as Uganda, Zaïre, and (in 1992) Kenya.

1985 Tens of thousands of Ethiopians go to Sudan to flee civil war and famine.

1988 Tens of thousands of Somalis flee as war breaks out in northwest Somalia. The Ethiopians who had been refugees in this area either return home or go to Kenya. By December 1990 there are 375,000 Somalis in Ethiopia.

1991 Refugees from southern Sudan are forced to leave Ethiopia after the fall of the Ethiopian leader, President Mengistu.
Fighting is widespread across Somalia. By 1992 one million people have fled to Kenya, Ethiopia, Djibouti, and Yemen.

1992 Ethiopian refugees in Kenya begin to return home.

1993 Some Somali refugees feel safe to return home in time to plant crops on their land.

Sudan The past

The name Sudan is short for Bilad as-Sudan which means "land of the black people." Originally, this was the name given to all black African countries south of the Sahara. It was only in the 19th century that the name Sudan came into use for the country we know today.

In ancient times, gold was mined in Sudan. The pharaohs (kings) of Egypt built settlements there to protect Upper Egypt, and to exploit the gold mines. Egypt's influence lasted many centuries, and during the 19th century Egypt established a network of provincial governments to keep control over Sudan. Sudanese attempts to become independent began early in the 1880s when an Islamic leader, the Mahdi (meaning "Messiah"), began a war to claim Sudan from the Egyptians and their British

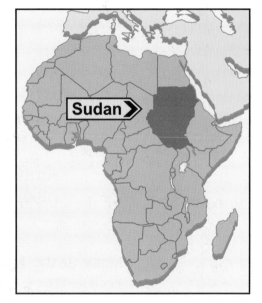

Sudan

rulers. The Mahdi managed to drive out both the Egyptians and the British, but these two powers later joined forces to regain Sudan. Their victory in 1898 resulted in joint British and Egyptian rule until independence in 1956.

Sudan is the largest country in Africa, and the ninth largest in the world. It is often considered to be divided into two parts — a northern, Muslim half and a southern half where people follow Christian or traditional African religions. When Sudan was a colony the two halves were ruled as separate territories, and since independence in 1956 there have been many problems between the people of northern and southern Sudan. The Arab (Muslim) north dominates the African (non-Muslim) south because it is richer and more developed. After independence,

civil war raged in the south, claiming an estimated 500,000 lives and forcing hundreds of thousands more people to leave their homes. The government of Sudan spent much of its money on weapons to fight the war, rather than on its starving and homeless people.

In 1969, Colonel Nimeri took over government and managed to end the civil war by promising the people of the south some independence from the north. An agreement made in 1972 paved the way for many refugees to return to southern Sudan. However, in 1983, Nimeri overturned this agreement and imposed strict Muslim laws upon the entire country. This led to the resumption of the civil war.

In the south, the Sudanese People's Liberation Army (SPLA) was formed, and it has been at war with the government of Khartoum (the capital of Sudan) since 1983. Since 1992, the SPLA itself has split into two groups that have been at war with one another. Hundreds of thousands of people have fled from Sudan

Sudan The present

into neighboring Ethiopia, Uganda and Kenya. People have also left their homes and traveled to other parts of Sudan. These refugees are known as displaced people, and they are often in an even worse plight than those who have left the country. Villages may be trapped by fighting, making the delivery of food supplies very difficult. Some areas are too dangerous for relief workers to enter, and often the only way to get food to displaced people is by dropping it from planes. No one knows how many displaced people are in Sudan — some estimates put it at nearly three million. Many are suffering from hunger and disease. Most are living on the brink of disaster, always ready to flee the next attack.

The situation in southern Sudan is still getting worse. The estimated three million displaced people trapped in Sudan could flood across the border to Uganda, Ethiopia, Zaïre, or Kenya at any time. But there are already 42,000 Sudanese refugees in Ethiopia, 28,000 in Kenya, 150,000 in Uganda, and 135,000 in Zaïre.

In 1988, relief workers in southern Sudan observed thousands of boys walking towards Ethiopia. They were coming from the western Upper Nile and Bahr el Gazal, hundreds of miles away. Already separated from their families by their jobs as cattle herders, these boys trekked east along the Nile and Sobat rivers until they reached Ethiopia. Most were fleeing attack from government troops. But as well as seeking peace and security, they were also leaving in order to go to school, as many of the schools in southern Sudan had been closed because of the war. Education is an important goal for these boys. Relief workers often reported seeing exhausted and starving boys clutching their only possessions — books.

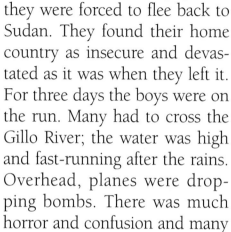

In the refugee camp at Panyido in Ethiopia, the Sudanese refugee boys lived in dormitories and were given the education and security that they longed for.

However, when the Mengistu government fell on May 27, 1991 (see page 47), they were forced to flee back to Sudan. They found their home country as insecure and devastated as it was when they left it. For three days the boys were on the run. Many had to cross the Gillo River; the water was high and fast-running after the rains. Overhead, planes were dropping bombs. There was much horror and confusion and many of the children were washed away and drowned.

Many of the boys settled for a while in Pochala and Nasir in southern Sudan. But there was always the threat of further attack, and they were soon moved to Narus. Here, food was scarce and even basic survival was difficult. In another attempt to provide safety for the boys, they were again moved to Kenya. After three months in a camp at Lokichokio, they arrived at their present home at Kakuma refugee camp in northwest Kenya.

Chol Paul Guet and his travels

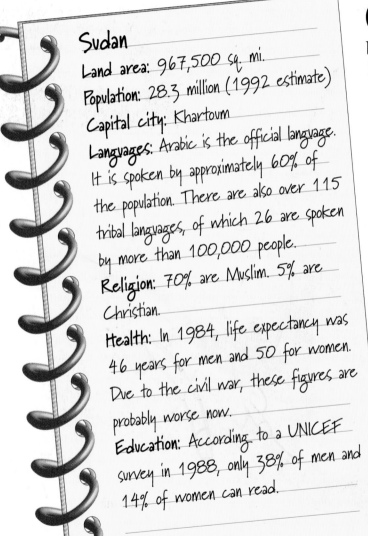

Sudan

Land area: 967,500 sq. mi.

Population: 28.3 million (1992 estimate)

Capital city: Khartoum

Languages: Arabic is the official language. It is spoken by approximately 60% of the population. There are also over 115 tribal languages, of which 26 are spoken by more than 100,000 people.

Religion: 70% are Muslim. 5% are Christian.

Health: In 1984, life expectancy was 46 years for men and 50 for women. Due to the civil war, these figures are probably worse now.

Education: According to a UNICEF survey in 1988, only 38% of men and 14% of women can read.

C hol comes from Sudan. He is a confident and independent boy, and unlike many of his friends he speaks good English and Swahili.

After I met him, Chol ran away from Kakuma to Nairobi, the capital of Kenya, for two weeks. He said he wanted to find a better education for himself. He returned because "Nairobi is a very dangerous place."

Chol was happy to talk about his walk from Sudan. It took a while to find out the "true" story, however, with some versions including heroic tales of fighting lions! Chol is one of many Sudanese children desperate to have a good education.

Chol Paul Guet, aged 14, Sudanese, Dinka Bor tribe.

Chol's journey

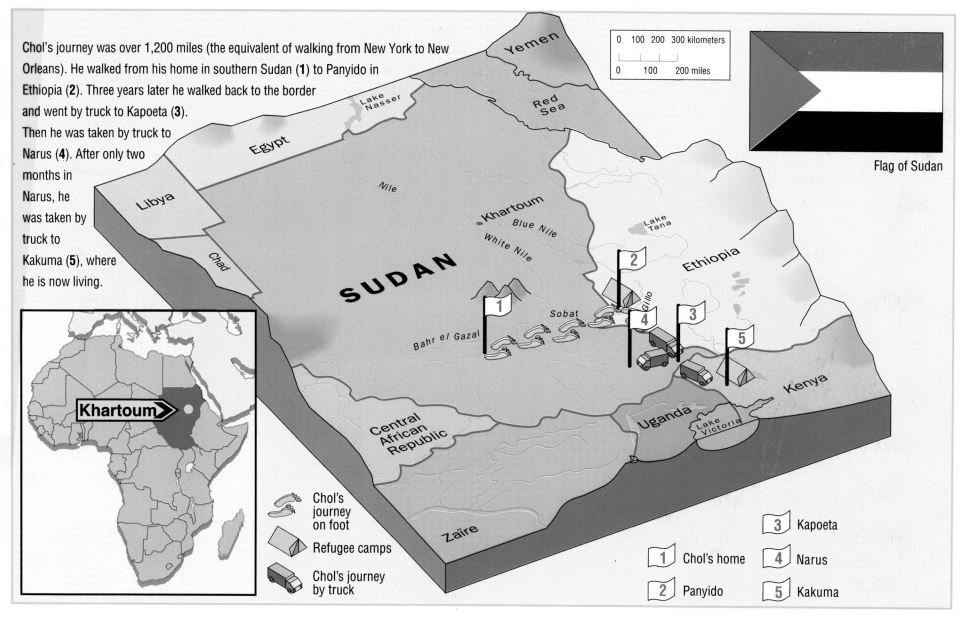

Chol's journey was over 1,200 miles (the equivalent of walking from New York to New Orleans). He walked from his home in southern Sudan (**1**) to Panyido in Ethiopia (**2**). Three years later he walked back to the border and went by truck to Kapoeta (**3**). Then he was taken by truck to Narus (**4**). After only two months in Narus, he was taken by truck to Kakuma (**5**), where he is now living.

Flag of Sudan

Chol's journey on foot

Refugee camps

Chol's journey by truck

1 Chol's home

2 Panyido

3 Kapoeta

4 Narus

5 Kakuma

Something like an accident

"It was something like an accident when I ran away from my village. We were playing at about 5 o'clock when these people, the soldiers, came. We just ran. We didn't know where we were going to, we just ran. The soldiers divided into two groups; one for the village, one for our herds of cattle. My brother helped me to run. We didn't know where our mother or father were, we didn't say goodbye. When there is shooting, when you hear BANG! BANG! BANG!, you don't think about your friend or your mother, you just run to save your life.

I didn't see the soldiers, I just heard the shooting, the screaming and the bombing that went DUM, DUM, DUM, DUM like this and killed many people. It all just happened, like an accident, and we ran without anything — nothing — no food, no clothes, nothing.

In the day the sun is hot and your feet burn. So we walked at night when it is cold, because then you don't say all the time, 'I want water, I want water.' To rest we stood under trees, but you can die of hunger if you give up and just lie under a tree.

Wild animals, lions, killed many people. You see, when you stay behind and say, 'I don't want to do this walking, this running, I just want to sit,' the lion will kill you. But I was not scared because I was with many people, and when the lion came we would shout, 'Huh! Huh! Go! Go!' and then the lion would not kill us.

"I was not scared because I was with many people."

16

So we just walked. We ate soil and the leaves of trees. The big boys knew the way. I think God showed us the way. You see, when you have God he says, 'Go this way' to the good people. But without God you could go this way, that way — and where do you go?

On the roads you can't leave a person who just sits down. You must pinch him and say, 'Get up! Get up!' God has told you that you must take this person, he is life. How did I keep walking? When I saw a small boy walking I would say, 'See this small boy? He is walking.' And I would carry on. We would tell stories to make us happy, saying, 'We are going to get food, we will be happy.'

We never felt well. We just walked.

On the roads you can't leave a person who just sits down. You must pinch him and say 'Get up! Get up!'

People died of hunger. I saw many dying. Even my friend died. There was no water, no food. When I saw my friend dying I carried on walking. You see sometimes you can help, and then sometimes you can't. You are talking about your life. I had to leave my friend because I would die with him. When he refuses, when he won't go, what can you do?

After, two months, we came to the Anyak tribe, who knew the way to Ethiopia. They helped us get fish and make dry fish. Not bad! We would catch the fish standing in the

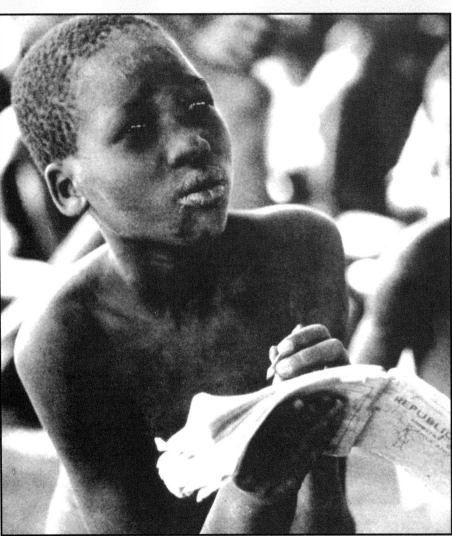

Desperate to learn

Something like an accident

Like children all over the world, refugee children enjoy playing dominoes.

river, but ten fish can't feed five million people, and everybody wanted some. So, we would catch and give to the next person. We stood in a line in the river. Sometimes, someone would take a fish and then run away with it. But what can you do?

To go to Ethiopia, to the Panyido refugee camp, there was a big river we had to swim across. Many people drowned on the way. Some people who did not know how to swim refused to go, saying, 'We could be going anywhere, to

Europe, anywhere!' When you have two or three brothers they can help. We try this way, that way, every way. There were strings and ropes to help pull people across. Many people stayed to teach themselves to swim. You see, you die if you can't swim. If the water goes over your head like this — whoosh — then you turn over and crash and die.

> **They gave us food, one hand like this, only one handful to last one week.**

In Panyido, we did not have food for two months, but at least there was peace. Some people tried to steal the sorghum from the village, but they had to be killed. Then the United Nations, he came, he saw the people, he went to Geneva to find food, and he came back. I spent three years in Ethiopia and felt well. I went to school and lived with five other boys. Then the United Nations left and we had to run. You see, the new president of Ethiopia did not want refugees. So he came and chased the refugees away. We couldn't do anything, what could we do? It was not our country.

So, we had to swim and then swim again. Some trucks took us from the border to Kapoeta town. It took two weeks. Sometimes we would have to wait for two days at a river. They gave us food, one hand like this, only one handful to last one week. And water, dirty water and we were sick, very sick with the diarrhea and the bump, bump of the road. At Kapoeta, after three days the United Nations said, 'Take them off to Narus.' What was happening we didn't know, when we asked people they said there was fighting and bombing and the soldiers might get us. In Narus we

The children of Kakuma camp, fascinated by the camera and the photographer

started building our schools and getting books, but we had to leave after only two months because of more fighting. You see, the United Nations High Commissioner for Refugees, he was in Kenya, not Sudan, so we went to Kenya where we would be safe.

Now I live with other boys in Kakuma. We cook for ourselves and build our own homes. I like playing basketball, but there is also football and school if you would like.

We are town people now, we have shoes and a shirt, you see? I say, let us stay here where it is safe. In England you are safe, now let us stay here safely. Now we want to learn. One day I will be an engineer to build Sudan like the other countries in Africa.

I don't know whether my mother and father are dead or alive. I was 9 when I left Sudan. I am 14 now. I am an oldie man now. My mother will not know me. **"**

The walking of the many

Painting by David Kumcieng, aged 15, Sudanese, Kakuma refugee camp.

"We wanted to run, but we had to walk because we were tired and so hot and hungry. In my picture the people are wearing clothes, but of course we didn't have any clothes. We saw people dying, it was always the young ones, the hungry ones and the old ones."

Crossing the River Gillo

Painting by Mac Anyat, aged 17, Sudanese, Kakuma refugee camp.

"It was terrible. People shouting, screaming: 'Run, swim, go, go!' Where was my friend? He was taken by the river. Nobody was anybody's friend. How can you be a friend when people are shooting at you and the river is going whoosh — and you have to go in that river? The bang, bang and the whoosh, whoosh made my mind go dead and I don't remember who was there, who died, what happened."

Tit for tat

The camel and the fox were friends and thieves. A true friendship. One day, they wanted to cross the river so that they could go to the farm and steal food. The camel said to the fox, "Get on my back so that we can cross the river." And the fox crossed the river on the camel's back.

On the other side, they arrived at the farm. The fox caught the chickens and the camel ate the vegetables. The fox finished eating the chickens quickly because he had only a small stomach. When he had finished, he said to the camel, "After I have eaten my lunch I am accustomed to singing."

The camel, who had not finished eating because he had a large stomach, cried, "Don't sing! The farmer will hear you. Let me finish my lunch first." But the fox didn't listen, and started to sing. The men at the farm heard the singing and came running. The fox ran away quickly, but the camel could only run slowly. The men caught the camel and beat him until his bones started to hurt. When they let him go he went to the river. The

fox was waiting there because he couldn't swim.

The fox said, "Can I get on your back to cross the river?"

The camel replied, "Get up!" and the fox jumped on to the camel's back. When the camel came to the middle of the river, where the water is very deep, he said, "After I have eaten my lunch, I am accustomed to taking a bath."

The fox begged, "No, no, please don't take a bath! I will drown!"

"I'm sorry," replied the camel, "but I always take a bath after lunch." And slowly he let his backbone go down into the water.

"Help!" shouted the fox.

The camel said, "Do you feel sorry for what you did?"

"Yes! Help!" replied the fox.

The camel felt sorry for the fox. He said, "I cannot let you die," and he took the fox to the other side of the river. When they reached the riverbank, the fox and the camel both promised that they would never hurt one another again. "But," said the camel, "that was tit for tat." And they both laughed.

by Daniel Arou Diing Arou
aged 14, Sudanese, Dinka Bor tribe.

Painting by Yel Awar Langar, aged 14, Sudanese, Kakuma refugee camp. "I hope that other children enjoy my stories. Sometimes I think that people think we don't laugh, we don't play. Of course we do!"

Kakuma refugee camp — the children's camp

In Kakuma refugee camp, there are 25,000 children in a camp of 40,000 people. Some of these children have not seen or heard from their parents for seven years. Almost all the children are boys between 7 and 15 years old, the girls having stayed behind in their villages in southern Sudan. The sad fact is that many of these boys have allegedly already served as child soldiers.

Kakuma is a very positive camp in which the boys' welfare and education is well provided for. Social workers have started a foster care project among the Sudanese refugees in the camp to give the boys some security. Another project to help the boys trace their parents in Sudan has also begun.

But refugee camps are not islands of peace. The political problems between the rival tribes that are fighting in Sudan are just as strong in the camp. The children feel tied to the war. For these boys, nightmares about their past experiences are made worse by their feelings of responsibility, and, sadly, many return to Sudan to fight as soon as they are old enough.

Some refugee workers are given bicycles for use around the camp. At the end of the day, their bicycles are in great demand.

◄ Laundry — a job everyone hates!

▼ Every day the boys take turns to line up for water. Another job everybody hates!

► The boys cook in groups of six. They are given wheat flour, cabbage, oil and sugar.

▼ Making bricks out of mud to build a house or a school.

◄ Having fun! Many refugees are quite used to seeing journalists and photographers in the camp and are not shy about showing off.

► Grinding wheat to make chapatis, a kind of flat bread

The party

Once upon a time, the animals decided that they would live in one group and the birds would live in another group. So, one day, the animals decided to have a party. The Zebra was the watchman. All the animals came to the party to have a happy time. Then the Bat arrived and said,

"Let me into the party, for I am an animal."

But the Zebra said, "No! We are animals because we don't have wings; you are a bird because you have wings."

So the bat left without going to the party.

The next day, the birds decided to have a party. The Vulture was the watchman of the bird party. The Bat heard the party from a long way away and decided he would go. When he arrived at the party he said,

"Let me into the party, for I am a bird."

But the Vulture said, "No! We are birds because we don't have teeth; you are an animal because you have teeth."

So the Bat had to leave without going to the party. The poor Bat was not an animal and not a bird, so he could never go to a party.

I say: tell the children of the world, we don't want to be bats. We want to find our place, to be either an animal or a bird so that we can be happy.

by Abraham Marial Kiol
aged 14, Sudanese, Dinka Bor tribe.

Painting by Zekaria Aken Deng, aged 15, Sudanese, Kakuma refugee camp.

Dinka man fighting buffalo

Painting by Simon Mac Anyuat, aged 17, Sudanese, Kakuma refugee camp.

"My picture shows a man from my tribe, the Dinka, wearing traditional clothes and fighting a buffalo to prove that he is a man."

My village in Sudan

Painting by Bor Alier, aged 17, Sudanese, Kakuma refugee camp.

"In my village in Sudan, people would come and take photographs of us and ask about our terrible life. We would tell them how we had lost our cattle, how we needed help. Then they would go away. Again and again. We thought they would help. Then one day we had to run. We had nothing. Nobody came back to help. Don't ask me about my problems. You will just go away too."

Somalia The past

During the Middle Ages, Arab merchants established trading posts in Somalia. These became Muslim centers and, as a result, most Somalis are Muslims. Most countries in Africa are made up of people from different tribes, speaking different languages. But Somalia is an exception. All Somalis share a common language, culture, and a belief that their Muslim leaders are descendants of Aquil Abu Talib, cousin of the prophet Muhammad. However, despite these common origins, the Somali people are still divided by clan rivalry. Somalia is divided into six clans, each containing many smaller groups or sub-clans. The main clans are: Dir, Darod, Isaq, Hawiya, Digil and Rahanwein.

Somalia was divided into European colonies at the end of the 19th century. One part went to the British to form the northern region of Kenya. Another went to France; it is now Djibouti. The Ogaden region was given to Ethiopia. The only parts left as Somalia after the division were Italian Somaliland, with its capital in Mogadishu, and British Somaliland, with its capital in Hargeisa.

In 1960, Italian Somaliland and British Somaliland became independent and united to form one nation. Since that time there has been a move to unify all the regions inhabited by Somali people to form a "Greater Somalia". The five territories containing Somali people are represented by the five points of the white star on the Somali flag.

The first government that was formed after independence had representatives from all the

Muslim children learn about the Koran, the Muslim holy book

clans. However, it soon became disrupted by clan problems, and in 1969 democratic rule came to an end when General Mohammed Siad Barre seized power.

In 1977, Somalia went to war with Ethiopia to try to regain the Ogaden region, but the Soviet Union (as it was then) helped Ethiopia to defeat Somalia. Hundreds of thousands of Somali people living in Ethiopia were forced to flee across the border to Somalia. An agreement between Somalia and Ethiopia in 1988 paved the way for these refugees to return home.

From the mid-1980s, rebel groups began to challenge the authority of President

Somalia The present

Siad Barre's government. The President responded by imprisoning, torturing and executing his opponents. In 1988, people in northwest Somalia were forced to flee as civil war broke out between rebel and government troops. By 1990 the fighting had spread to the capital, Mogadishu, and in 1991 Siad Barre fell from power. One of the rebel groups declared their leader president. The other rebel groups immediately rejected this.

Since November 1991, the fighting in Somalia has been taking place between the various Somali groups in a struggle for power. Thousands of people have been killed in this savage civil war. Late in November 1992, the Secretary General of the United Nations (UN) decided that it was necessary to send UN troops to restore peace in Somalia. The first American troops arrived on December 9, 1992. Unfortunately, the UN troops also became targets for the rebel Somali groups. But by mid-1993 the situation in some parts of Somalia had improved enough for some people to be able to return home.

As a result of the civil war, almost one million people from all over Somalia have been forced to flee to Kenya, Djibouti, Yemen, and Ethiopia. Those that went to Kenya traveled by boat or car, or they walked. Some refugees from Mogadishu walked for up to 90 days in incredible heat to reach the Kenyan border. Many survived only by eating leaves from trees. Sadly, many died on the way.

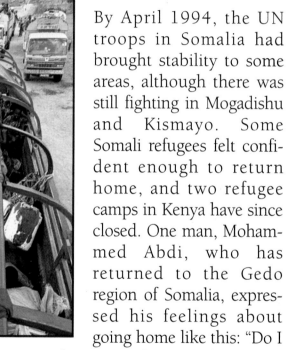

It is hard to say who was worst affected by the refugee crisis. Most Somalis left their homes in a hurry, with no time to collect possessions or say goodbye to friends. Many families were split up and still live in the hope that they will one day be reunited. For the elderly it was particularly difficult. As one tired, starved, and depressed woman explained: "It is hard that I have lost my family, my home, and my land. Now I arrive in Kenya. I have no clothes, I have to ask for my food, my shelter. I have lost my dignity."

By April 1994, the UN troops in Somalia had brought stability to some areas, although there was still fighting in Mogadishu and Kismayo. Some Somali refugees felt confident enough to return home, and two refugee camps in Kenya have since closed. One man, Mohammed Abdi, who has returned to the Gedo region of Somalia, expressed his feelings about going home like this: "Do I want to be in my home village? Of course I do. Living in a refugee camp is like living in a prison; you are given your food and shelter, but nothing else. You go mad just sitting. You spend your whole time dreaming of going home."

God is the greatest

Both paintings by Aden Ahmed Mohid, aged 14, Somali, Dagahaley refugee camp.

"We Somali children are Muslims. We go to Koranic school to learn about Islam. Here we stand in a circle singing inside our school."

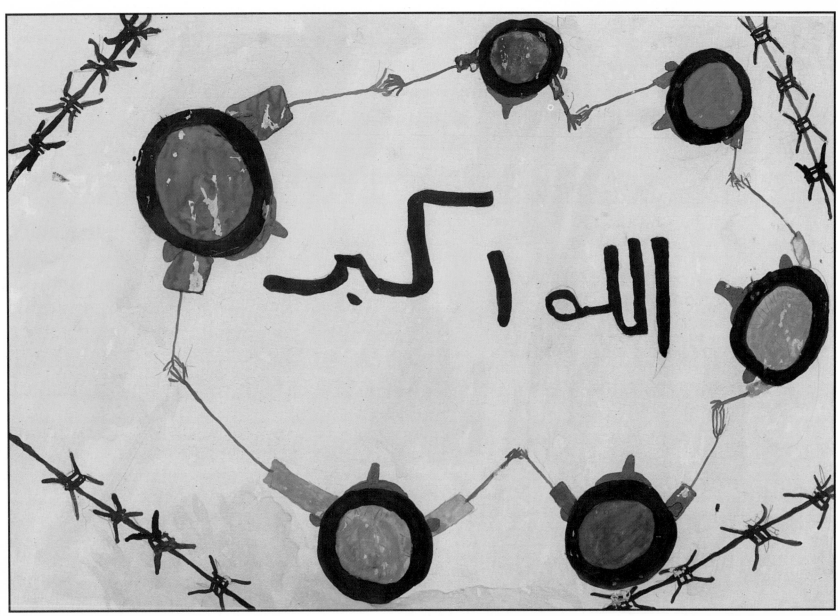

Walking to Kenya

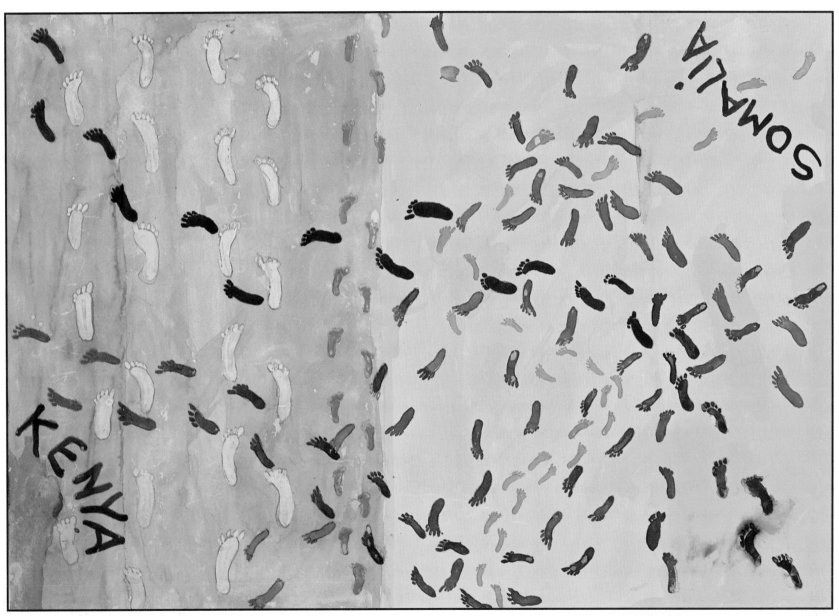

Shukri Jania Ebrahim and her travels

Somalia

Land area: 246,200 sq. mi.

Population: 7.2 million (1992 estimate)

Capital city: Mogadishu

Languages: mainly Somali

Religion: 99% are Muslim

Health: In 1990 average life expectancy was 46 years for men and women. About 13% of infants die. According to the World Bank, health standards are among the worst in Africa, and due to the famine and the war these figures are probably worse now.

Education: In 1972 the first Somali script was introduced. According to a UNICEF survey in 1980, only 18% of men and 6% of women can read and write.

Shukri comes from Somalia. When I first met her, she was with a large group of Somali women. She looked much older than 15. She was helping her mother to cook.

Shukri's mother is very reliant on her. While they lived in Nairobi, Shukri went to school. But now she stays at home to look after her mother.

The Somali women stick together for protection. They feel very vulnerable without the support of men.

Shukri Jania Ebrahim, aged 15, Somali, Haweia clan.

Shukri's journey

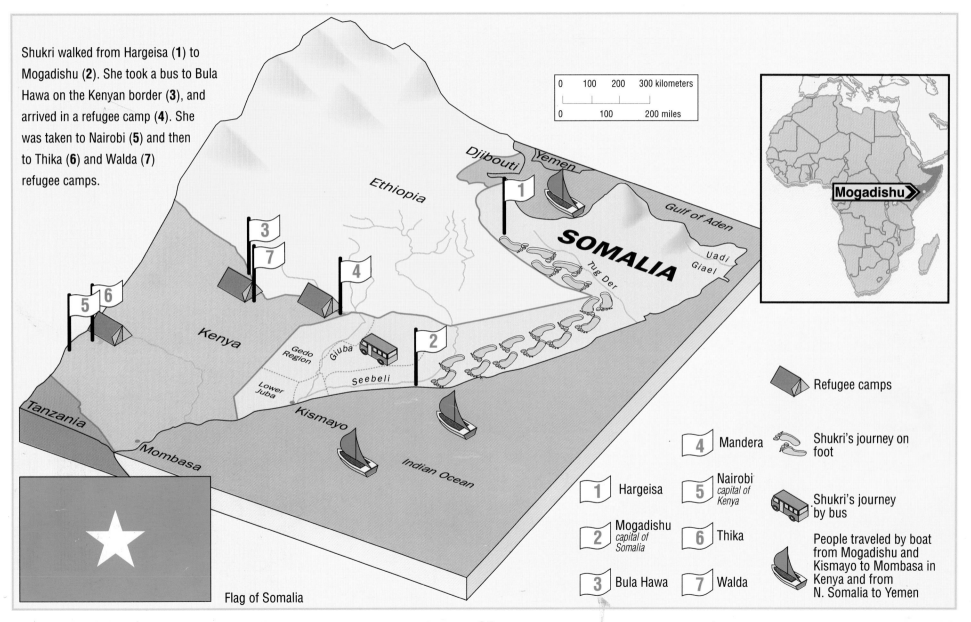

Shukri walked from Hargeisa (**1**) to Mogadishu (**2**). She took a bus to Bula Hawa on the Kenyan border (**3**), and arrived in a refugee camp (**4**). She was taken to Nairobi (**5**) and then to Thika (**6**) and Walda (**7**) refugee camps.

0   100   200   300 kilometers
0   100   200 miles

Djibouti   Yemen

Ethiopia

Gulf of Aden

SOMALIA

Uadi Giael

Tug Der

Mogadishu

Kenya

Gedo Region   Giuba

Lower Juba   Seebeli

Tanzania

Mombasa   Kismayo

Indian Ocean

Flag of Somalia

Refugee camps

4 Mandera   Shukri's journey on foot

1 Hargeisa   **5** Nairobi *capital of Kenya*   Shukri's journey by bus

2 Mogadishu *capital of Somalia*   **6** Thika   People traveled by boat from Mogadishu and Kismayo to Mombasa in Kenya and from N. Somalia to Yemen

3 Bula Hawa   **7** Walda

I am the firstborn

"We were among the first Somali refugees to come to Kenya. We used to live in Hargeisa which is in northern Somalia. My father was a very rich man; we lived in a villa. My father's clan is the Haweia. I think you know General Aideed who comes from my clan?

After 15 days at sea, a sailing boat arrives in Mombasa harbour. Crammed aboard are 378 hungry, thirsty, and frightened refugees from Somalia.

One day, some men came to my house. They were not soldiers; they were dressed like you and me. They asked the last-born child, who was only four years old, 'Is father in?' When my father heard it was them, he took me into another room and told me, 'These men have come looking for Somali National Movement people. They think I am one of them. This will be the last time I see you. Now you are the mother and the father.'

He gave me some papers that he said I should give to my mother so that she could get money from the people in town. Then my father met those men. My father told them, 'I will come with you. I don't want any fighting in front of my children.'

I asked the men, 'Are you taking him for good?' They told me, 'No, no, we are just going for a meeting.' I was the last person in my family to see my father.

> They told me, "No, no, we are just going for a meeting." I was the last person in my family to see my father.

The fighting was horrible. The government was looking for people belonging to the rebel group, the Somali National Movement; they were killing people, raping girls. Nobody cared because everybody was trying to save their own lives. We could not trust anybody as they were all scared of us because of father. Three days after they took father, Mama decided that we should leave Hargeisa and go to Kenya. I am the firstborn, so I am responsible. We are nine children, three from my aunt who died. My Mama cannot live without me.

The first day of walking was normal for us, except that the sun made our legs feel swollen and awful. By the second day we were walking only at night because during the day the enemy was fighting and there were roadblocks on the road. It was the first time we had ever walked at night. We heard lions roaring, and we saw many snakes and scorpions. We didn't have any problems with the animals, though; it was the people we were scared of. Some boys from Hargeisa walked with us. They had money and helped us to carry the little children. After three days, they bought two donkeys and the little children sat on the donkeys. Myself, I had to walk because I am the firstborn. I used to put my feet in water when we reached a village at the end of the day. I would just fall down.

On the fourth day, my Mama became seriously ill. She was pregnant. Before, at home, she had to have an operation when she gave birth. She was in a lot of pain and we didn't know what to do. Luckily, a family in a Land Rover helped us. They took Mama in the car to Mogadishu and said that we must follow on our own. It took two days for us to walk to Mogadishu. They were very long days for me. If Mama died, then I had to look after all the children, and I didn't know where Kenya was.

I didn't know where Kenya was.

When we arrived in Mogadishu, the boys took us to the hospital where Mama was. She told us that her baby had died. She was very tired and had to spend one week in the hospital. We stayed with relatives of the boys. I stayed with the three youngest at one place, and the other children stayed at another. After one week, Mama came out of the hospital. The doctors told her she must not walk or carry heavy things. But we had no home in Mogadishu, so what could she do? People gave us money, saying that we should go back home. We said, 'Yes, yes, yes,' and took the money to get a bus to Kenya. How could we go home?

People were very kind to us. When we were walking to Mogadishu, people in the ▶ p39

▲ The Somalian refugees build their own homes, which are called tukuls.
◀ A refugee camp in north-eastern Kenya. About 45,000 Somalis live here.

Traveling to the refugee camp

Painting by Binti
Aden Denle, aged
12, Ethiopian, Ifo
refugee camp.

villages gave us milk and meat. In Mogadishu, when we asked for help, people gave us money.

We took a bus to Bula Hawa, on the border with Kenya. By this time my bones were aching. I thought I was going to die. We were taken in a truck to Mandera refugee camp and I went with my mother to the hospital. I had malaria, and my mother had stomach pains from her baby. The people in Mandera said it was very serious and we were transferred to Nairobi. We cried until all my brothers and sisters came, too.

> **By this time my bones were aching. I thought I was going to die.**

We stayed in Nairobi for three years at Thika refugee camp. I went to school, where I learned English. In 1992, we were transferred to Walda refugee camp. By this time, there were many Somali

Somali refugees traveling by truck

refugees in Kenya because the country was totally messed up. We didn't like Walda, it was like a desert, but the people said that we must go to Walda so that we could plan for the future, so that we could be resettled. You see, we cannot go back to Somalia. People hate us in Somalia, and we have no home, no family, no nothing.

Last month, we heard news of my father. They put him in a hole for two years with no

I am the firstborn

light so that he became blind. He was with eight other men. When the fighting became very serious in 1992 they stopped feeding him properly. When he came out of the hole, the woman told me he had scars all over his body. He died last month.

I am the firstborn and I feel very sad. Life here is very hard. The life in Somalia was very different. This place is a jungle place. Even the way we looked before and the way we look now is dif-

> **I am the firstborn and I feel very sad. Life here is very hard.**

ferent. I have a problem with the boys here. I will not get married or have a boyfriend because my Mama needs me. I don't think my Mama would survive without me. I have to look after my family first. I will feel threatened as long as I am without a father or brother to protect me.

I would like to tell you that my story is not the same for all Somalis. There were many who came to Kenya in 1992 when the fighting was very bad. They were starving and very sick. We were lucky, people helped us. But these people did not have anyone to ask for help. 99

Women fight hard for their survival, and for that of their children. Without husbands or fathers to protect them, they are vulnerable to attack.

A food drop

Painting by David Deng Aleu, aged 16, Sudanese, Kakuma refugee camp.

"Everybody is happy about the food drop. I am watching. A blind lady is being helped by a small boy. People are jumping to catch food."

The deaf man and the blind man

Once upon a time there were two men, one deaf and one blind, who lived in the same town. One day there was fighting and the people of the town decided to move to another place. The deaf man saw everyone leaving, but didn't understand why. The blind man heard everybody leaving, but couldn't follow. They were both left feeling very sad.

Some people told the blind man where to go, but he didn't know how to follow his people because he didn't have any eyes. The deaf man couldn't hear the instructions of how to follow his people.

The blind man called for help, but the deaf man could not hear him. Luckily the deaf man saw the blind man. He took his hand, and using hand language they worked out where the people had gone. When they arrived in the town, the king saw them. He was amazed when he heard their story, and promised that they would never be left again.

by Batula Mohammed Ali aged 13, Somali.

Painting by Zekana Alien Deng, aged 15, Sudanese, Kakuma refugee camp.

Sailing from Kismayo

Both paintings by Said Abdi Said, aged 14, Somali, Dagahaley refugee camp.

"I lived in Kismayo until the fighting became very bad. Then I left with my mother, brothers, and sisters. We had to pay to go on this boat with many, many other people. At night we were cold with the wind and during the day we were burnt by the sun. It should have been fun, but the old people were sick and we were leaving our home behind. For one day, OK — but two weeks...!"

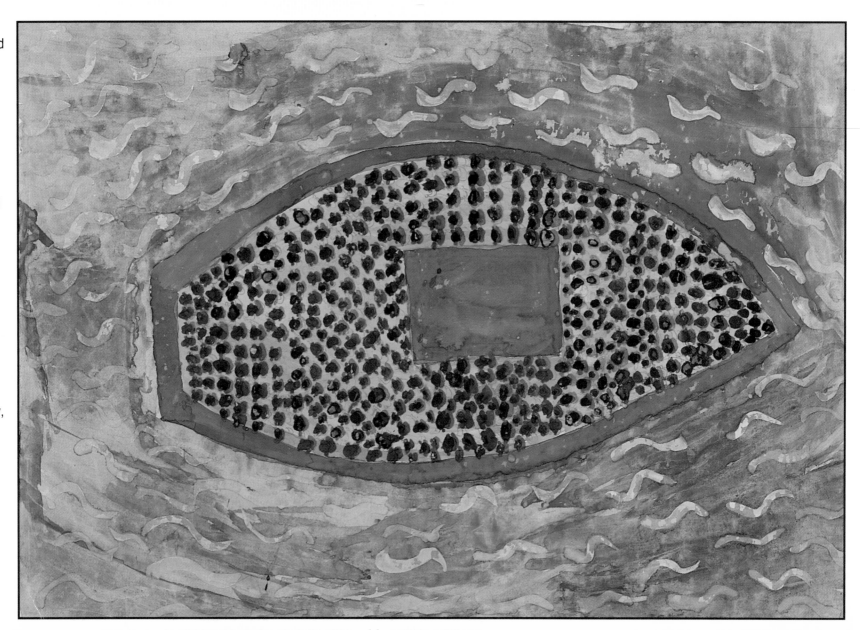

"When we arrived in Mombasa we had to wait to be allowed into the country. It was terrible. I know that nobody wants refugees, but do they know that we don't want to be refugees?"

Ethiopia The past

Ethiopia has one of the richest and oldest histories in Africa. One legend says that the first Ethiopian ruler, Menelik, was a descendant of King Solomon of Israel and the Queen of Sheba. During ancient Greek times, Ethiopia was thought to be the place where the sun set. Throughout its history, high mountains have protected Ethiopia from attack by other countries. The first invasion that the Ethiopians experienced was by the Italians, in 1895. The Italian army was defeated but Italy kept some territory in the coastal area of Eritrea.

In 1935, the situation changed when Italy finally conquered Ethiopia. The emperor of Ethiopia, Haile Selassie, was forced to live in exile in Britain until, in 1941, British, Indian, and Ethiopian troops drove out the Italians, and

Ethiopia became an independent country once again. However, the British ruled Eritrea until 1952, when an agreement was made to join the territory with Ethiopia. Under the terms of this agreement, Eritrea kept its own regional government.

Emperor Haile Selassie was killed by a group of army officials who took power in 1974. In 1977, Colonel Mengistu Haile Mariam became head of state and introduced a Communist government that was supported by the (then) Soviet Union. During his years in power, Mengistu built up a huge army and dealt ruthlessly with anyone who dared to question his government. Once, when a member of the government tried to question a policy at a meeting, Mengistu pulled out a gun and shot him on the spot. The whole country lived in

terror; over 100,000 people were killed, and thousands more escaped to neighboring countries.

In the late 1970s, Ethiopia and Somalia started to fight over the Ogaden region. Hundreds of thousands of Somalis living in the region were forced to flee as refugees to Somalia. Backed by the Soviet Union, Ethiopia won the war.

During Mengistu's rule, and after, three rebel groups were active in campaigning against the government. Eritrea was made a province of Ethiopia in 1962, going against the agreement made for regional government in 1952. This led to the formation of the Eritrean People's Liberation Front (EPLF). A second opposition group, the Tigrayan People's Liberation Front (TPLF) fought for greater freedom in dealing with the affairs of the region of Tigray. The third group formed was the Oromo Liberation Front (OLF) in the south of Ethiopia.

Ethiopia suffered from serious droughts

Ethiopia The present

in 1973-4, 1983-5, 1987, and 1989-90. Civil war helped to turn these droughts into famines. Regions seen as rebel areas by the government were deprived of aid. The famine in 1983-5 came to the world's attention following a news report on television. Pop stars, led by Bob Geldof, took part in the "Live Aid" concerts to raise money for aid for Ethiopia.

In May 1991, the Mengistu government was overthrown, and by July a new government was formed that included representatives from all the various movements in Ethiopia. At the same time, the EPLF formed a government in Eritrea and, in April 1993, Eritrea was pronounced an independent state. However, in Ethiopia disagreement about regional elections in June 1992 led to the OLF withdrawing from the state council. Fighting in southern Ethiopia followed, and many Oromo people fled to Kenya. An agreement between the Oromo and the government in November 1993 meant that these refugees could begin to return home.

M ost of the 75,000 Ethiopian refugees living in Kenya returned home at the end of 1993. However, there are still about 5,000 Ethiopian refugees in Kenya, many living in Kakuma camp. Most of them are "political" refugees who claim that their lives would be threatened if they returned to Ethiopia. Many are interested in resettling in Europe or the USA. But every year, fewer refugees are accepted by Western countries. This means that most of the Ethiopian refugees living in Kenya will stay there until they feel safe to return to Ethiopia.

Until that time, the Ethiopian refugees in Kakuma have established their own community. It is interesting to see the way that, with exactly the same equipment, the Ethiopians build their homes in a totally different way from the Sudanese. Many Ethiopian homes have "front rooms" built to provide a space for a shop. The Ethiopian quarter of Kakuma is the commercial center of the camp. Here, there are shops, shoemakers, and a "Hotel

Eritreans celebrating their independence in April 1993

Intercontinental," where the Ethiopian refugees provide the entertainment.

Many of the Ethiopian refugees are professional, educated people. In Kakuma, they feel very frustrated. As one woman explained: "I fled from Ethiopia as a student. Now I am in Kakuma, in this heat, with no books and no work to do. I feel like I am wasting my life."

Nebiyou Assefa and his travels

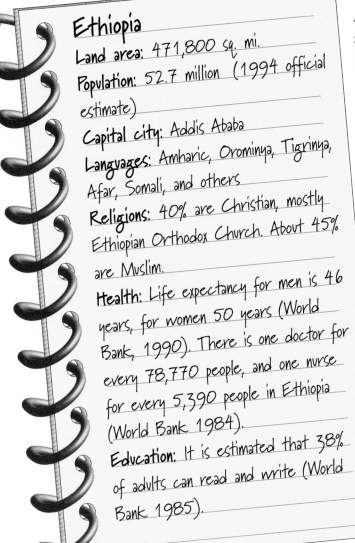

Ethiopia
Land area: 471,800 sq. mi.
Population: 52.7 million (1994 official estimate)
Capital city: Addis Ababa
Languages: Amharic, Orominya, Tigrinya, Afar, Somali, and others
Religions: 40% are Christian, mostly Ethiopian Orthodox Church. About 45% are Muslim.
Health: Life expectancy for men is 46 years, for women 50 years (World Bank, 1990). There is one doctor for every 78,770 people, and one nurse for every 5,390 people in Ethiopia (World Bank 1984).
Education: It is estimated that 38% of adults can read and write (World Bank 1985).

Nebiyou comes from Ethiopia. He is a shy boy with a good sense of humor. When I first met him he was painting in his hut. He was very bored because he had not yet been admitted to school.

Nebiyou lives with 42 other orphans. They have their own football team and music band. When I last visited him, I arranged for him to start carpentry lessons.

Nebiyou Assefa, aged 14, Ethiopian.

Nebiyou's journey

Nebiyou's route was from Addis Ababa (**1**) to Blate (**2**) with his father in a car. He went from Blate to Walda (**3**) in an army truck, and from Walda to Kakuma (**4**) in a UNHCR vehicle.

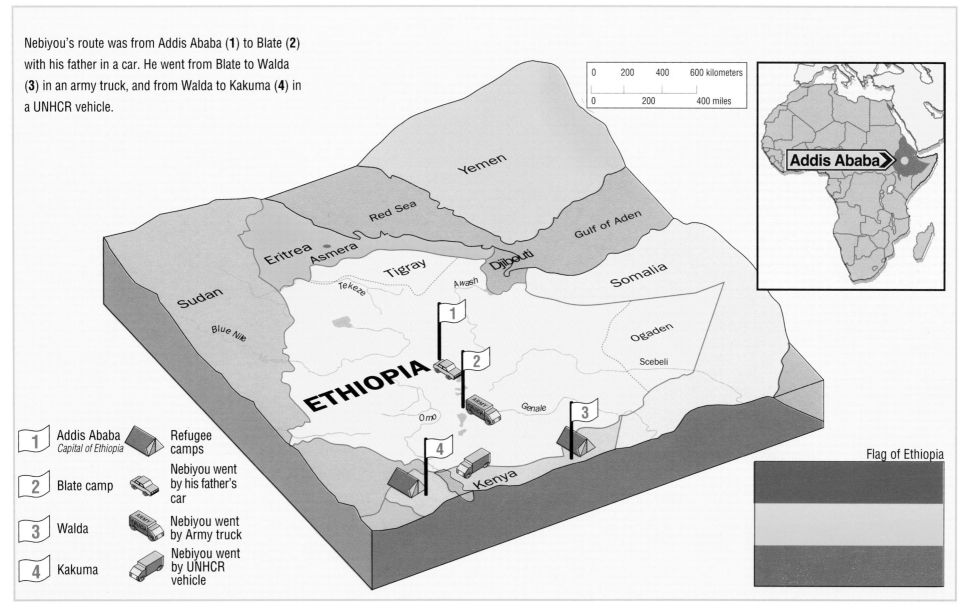

Flag of Ethiopia

1 Addis Ababa *Capital of Ethiopia*	Refugee camps
2 Blate camp	Nebiyou went by his father's car
3 Walda	Nebiyou went by Army truck
4 Kakuma	Nebiyou went by UNHCR vehicle

Who cares anyway?

"My name is Nebiyou Assefa; Nebiyou for me, Assefa for my father. I am 13, no, 14 — well, who cares anyway? When I lived in Ethiopia I lived with my father who was a soldier in a military camp. Well, of course, I didn't always live there; I lived in Addis Ababa with my mother until she died when I was small. In Addis I lived in a house with toys and such happy things. When my mother died, my father came and said, 'Now you will live with me.' So we went to Blate military camp. You know it? I think it is very famous.

It is difficult for me to tell you about my life in Ethiopia because it was a long time ago. My father said to me, 'You eat, you go to school, and you sleep,' and I was happy just to play

Ethiopian refugees traveling by bus in Kenya

A market scene in Ethiopia

and be with my father. Then, I don't know, one day he went to the fighting place. From that time he didn't come back. A soldier told me, 'If he live, I don't know: if he die, I don't know.' Think of the soldier telling me this news just like that! I said that this is big news and there is a big differ-

I had no mother, no father, no friend even.

ence if my father is dead or alive. But, you see, at the same time President Mengistu was sent from the country. Everybody listened to the radio all the time, and the whole community, it was changed. I walked around everywhere looking into doors. Nobody cared. Everything was messy, cars were driving everywhere. People were afraid of one another, and nobody wanted to look after me.

The soldiers said that this was very bad, that they had to go to Kenya to the refugee camps. I said, 'If they have to go, I have to go too.' You see, I had no mother, no father, no friend even. So it was by

chance that I came to Kenya. Of course, I didn't know how to get to Kenya, I didn't even know which direction it was in. ▶ p54

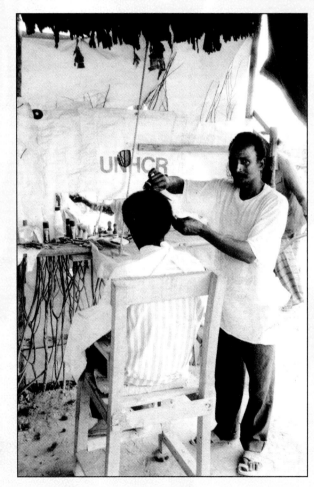

Having a haircut in the refugee camp

Ask the big people why

Painting by Liban Ahmed Habib, aged 10, Ethiopian, Ifo refugee camp.

"Don't ask me why I am a refugee, I don't know. Before we came here we lived with our camels. Now we live in a refugee camp. Soon we go home again. That is all — ask the big people why."

Children's faces in tents

Painting by Binti Aden Denle, aged 12, Ethiopian, Ifo refugee camp.

"All night we wait in tents for the day to come. This place is very dangerous, bandits attack us at night. I am showing the frightened faces of the children in our camp."

Who cares anyway?

I just heard people with families and soldiers talking about going to Kenya, and I knew that I must go too.

I came to Kenya in a big car. I wore a uniform and guns like the soldiers, and lay on the floor all the time. I wanted to live with them in the refugee camp in Kenya, but I am just a little boy and they said I had to live in the orphanage camp with the other orphan children.

We stayed in a refugee camp called Walda. Very soon, people did not like it because it was like living in a desert. So, so hot. You cannot think, you cannot eat, you cannot move. Other children were

Binti painting (see paintings pages 38 and 53)

lucky – they had a family, so when it was safe to go home they left with their families. They were happy to leave the desert. But us orphans? What about us? All that we could do was watch people go home and ask when we were going too. Our problem is that we love our country and want to return home. But we don't have parents, and because of that we can't go home.

Our refugee camp was closed and we were moved to a new camp called

Our problem is that we don't have parents and because of that we can't go home.

Kakuma. It was very bad when we arrived in the new camp. It was raining all the time and we did not have time to build a new home. People came and took our photographs to send to the government in Ethiopia. They said we could go home if someone from our family saw the photograph in Ethiopia. But we are orphans, we have no family, so what are we going to do? I feel simply left here.

We do not want to go to a place without friends. I have a friend called Beruke Meles who is also an orphan. I will go any place with him. I cook for Beruke and he cooks for me. We only want to learn now. Firstly, I want to learn and secondly, if I can do it, I want to do the doctor's work. If I cannot learn that way, I will do something so that I can live in my own country. **"**

The wise and the foolish

In traditional Ethiopian society, bible students (Yekolo Temari) were known for their wisdom, as well as for their tricks and mischievousness. The bible students were always young men. They often lived with poor priests, so they had to find cunning ways to get food and money. Although the students were often troublesome, they were considered to be symbols of the future and of new ideas. They were responsible for not allowing Ethiopia to get stuck in its traditional old ways.

Once upon a time, there were two friends. One was a fool, and one was wise. They were both very poor. One day, the wise one decided to leave his home in search of fortune.

"I am tired of having no clothes and no food," he told his foolish friend.

After a few hours of walking, the wise one became hungry. His rumbling stomach made him start thinking about how he was going to find food. He went to the riverside, caught a frog and put it in his pocket. He soon reached a town. He went straight to the best restaurant in town and ordered the biggest meal on the menu. At the end of the meal, he ordered a bowl of soup. When it arrived and the waiter was not looking, he put the frog into the soup. Then he shouted,

"Waiter, waiter, there's a frog in my soup!"

The owner of the restaurant heard him shouting and begged him to be quiet.

"You will ruin me!" he whispered to the wise one. "I will pay you if you don't tell anyone."

So the wise one left the restaurant with a full stomach and full pockets.

When the wise one arrived home, the foolish one saw that his wise friend was wearing new clothes. As soon as the foolish one heard how his friend had made his fortune, he decided that he was going to do the same. He walked to the same town, finding a frog on the way. When he reached the town he went to the same restaurant and ordered the same meal. At the end of the meal he asked for a bowl of soup.

"There is no more soup," said the waiter.

"This is terrible!" the foolish one shouted. "Where am I going to put my frog?"

The owner of the restaurant heard him, and was very angry. The foolish one was beaten and sent from the town.

by Girma Tescaye, aged 14, Ethiopian.

Postscript: Rwanda 1994

On April 28, 1994, over 200,000 people fled from Rwanda in Central Africa to neighboring Tanzania. They fled in fear of the violence between tribes which had killed an estimated 500,000 people in Rwanda in only one month. The border that they crossed was left open while the two warring armies fought for control of the region. For miles and miles, people could be seen walking through the torrential rain, but after 24 hours, when the area had been secured by the Rwandan Patriotic Front army, the border was closed.

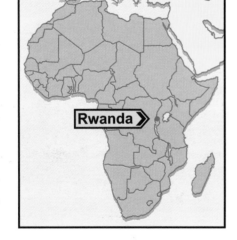

Men, women, and children from all walks of life joined the human chain of refugees crossing into Tanzania. People came on foot, on bicycle, and packed into trucks and cars. They carried only the bare essentials of life. As the rain poured down, they were forced to try to create a shelter out of their meager possessions. This was particularly frightening for the 1,000 children who had become separated from their families in the rush to escape from Rwanda.

Suddenly a refugee camp was Tanzania's second largest city. Relief workers struggled to provide help. Then, in July, a new wave of refugees fled Rwanda. Some 1.2 million people crossed into Zaïre in just two weeks. At the town of Goma, where most of the camped, there was not enough food, shelter, or clean water. Without clean water and latrines, cholera and other deadly diseases spread rapidly. A huge international relief effort was launched, with millions of dollars in government and private funds. U.S. soldiers went to help distribute the aid. Still, by late July, when the refugees began to go home, thousands had died.

In 1994 hundreds of thousands of people fled from Rwanda into Tanzania and Zaïre, creating a refugee crisis.

The United Nations High Commissioner for Refugees — UNHCR

"There is no greater sorrow on earth than the loss of one's native land."
—Euripides, 431 B.C.

Young children often flee from their homes without knowing why they are going or where they are going.

In 1970 there were 2.5 million refugees in the world. In 1984 there were 11 million. In 1994 the number was 19 million, more than half being children. Helping the world's millions of refugees is the job of the United Nations High Commissioner for Refugees (UNHCR), which was founded in 1951.

Wars, persecution, and intolerance have always produced refugees. But the increasing number of refugees is a reflection of the instability of the world in which we live. The stories of Chol, Shukri, and Nebiyou in this book echo the fate of numerous other children in wars raging around the world today. Children are often the main victims of war. They are killed and maimed during indiscriminate attacks on civilian communities. They also suffer from famine, malnutrition, disease, and the trauma of being separated from their families. Those who survive are likely to be scarred for life.

Forced to flee from their homes out of fear for their lives, refugees often give up everything: home, belongings, family, and coun-

try. They face an uncertain future in a strange land among people who do not always understand them. As a first priority, UNHCR gives protection to people from physical harm and from being forced to return to their own land. Relief assistance such as food, water, shelter, and medical care is also provided. The children, the

Food distribution

The United Nations High Commissioner for Refugees – UNHCR

single women, the elderly, and the disabled require special care.

Refugees are people just like you and me who, through no fault of their own, have been caught up in major upheavals. They are doctors and lawyers, farmers and fishermen, mothers, fathers, and children. Albert Einstein and Sigmund Freud were refugees. What if the world had turned its back on them? Most refugees dream of returning with dignity and safety to live in their own country. When the longed-for day arrives, the UNHCR helps refugees to go home and to stop being refugees. But when the situation in their home country makes it impossible to return, people can remain as refugees for a long time. Only a very small number of refugees are accepted every year to move permanently to a new country.

In a world where persecution, massive human rights violations, and armed conflict remain daily realities, the need to protect refugees is greater than ever before. Asylum for those who flee must be preserved.

Refugee houses

▲ An Ethiopian mud hut

◄ A Sudanese hut

▲ A Somalian tukul

The United Nations High Commissioner for Refugees supplies all refugees in Kenya with the same materials for building their homes. However, the final buildings look very different from one another, as the pictures above illustrate.

Save the Children

In a world where children are too often innocent victims of violence and natural disasters, the work of Save the Children is needed more than ever. In nearly 20 U.S. states and 40 nations, Save the Children's mission is to make lasting, positive changes in the lives of children. Save the Children believes that the best way to do this is to help people help themselves. That belief is the foundation of Save the Children emergency programs.

The emergency work of Save the Children ensures the survival of children while helping parents to rebuild their lives. With this approach, Save the Children encourages a return to self-sufficiency while meeting the immediate needs of children and their families. Recent emergency programs have included relief efforts for war-related crises in Africa; comprehensive response programs for natural disasters in Asia; and aid to victims of conflict in the Middle East and Eastern Europe. Refugee resettlement and repatriation programs are operated in cooperation with World Education and World Learning for Cambodian, Lao, and Vietnamese refugees. Ongoing efforts have helped children traumatized by war in Southern Africa, Rwanda, and Bosnia. Along with emergency response programs, Save the Children promotes health care, education, and economic programs.

Through the International Save the Children Alliance, a worldwide confederation of independent organizations, Save the Children is part of efforts around the globe. For example, in Rwanda in 1994, Save the Children provided support and assistance to the work of Save the Children Fund of the United Kingdom and the United Nations High Commissioner for Refugees, while operating its own programs for traumatized Rwandan children.

Working for the Swedish Save the Children Fund (also a member of ISCA), Rädda Barnen runs a number of programs for the unaccompanied children in Kakuma refugee camp, northwest Kenya. One of the priorities of these programs is to try to give back to the children their lost sense of security, discipline, and responsibility. Adult refugees in the camp are recruited as supervisors for groups of up to 40 children. Their task is to encourage the children to be self-sufficient. In groups of six they build their own homes, cook their food, and keep their living area clean and neat.

The Swedish Save the Children is also continuing the painting project set up by Sybella Wilkes and Sironka Averdung. Many refugee children suffer from forms of anxiety that they are more easily able to express through painting than in words. The project is a good example of the efforts being made by Save the Children to give children the opportunity to work through their problems and experiences in order that the rest of the world may try to understand and help.

Using this book in school

In the 1980s and 1990s hundreds of thousands of people have fled from their homes in the Horn of Africa, and the movement of refugees is likely to be one of the great moral and political challenges of the next century — a challenge for which young people must be prepared.

One day we had to run!, by use of its testimonies and cultural material, shows the effects of wars, environmental degradation and the abuse of human rights on the lives of ordinary children. Teachers can use the material in this book to enable students to explore concepts such as migration, justice, human rights, safety, and the experience of being a newcomer. In particular, it can be used to teach skills and concepts as suggested below.

Whole school learning

The experiences of having to move recounted by the children in this book could be presented at school assemblies where the theme is homelessness, migration, or refugees. The firsthand testimonies and illustrations could also add an African dimension to group sessions with the aim of broadening the everyday experiences of young people. In this way, the book is a useful tool for strengthening the human rights ethos of schools.

Curriculum-focused learning

The broad areas outlined here are directly applicable to the requirements of school curricula.

For **geography**, this book provides authentic material to support lessons structured around themes of population movement, environmental protection, and economic development. Close study of how and why children and families had to leave their homes in southern Sudan to flee to northern Kenya can involve mapwork skills as well as picture and discussion work on transportation, homes, and domestic economies.

For **history**, the colonial frontiers and the names of the countries in the Horn of Africa support work on wider world themes such as pre- and post-colonial African history, and larger movements of people over time.

For **religion**, the moral dilemmas related to war, violence and children's rights can be discussed through learning about the real experiences of children in difficult circumstances in one area of Africa. The situation in the Horn of Africa also provides scope for gaining an understanding of Christianity and Islam, and the interaction between these two major world faiths.

For **language**, the use of the children's own words adds to any exploration on the theme of childhood, or topic work on homes and journeys. Group discussion exercises could be devised to draw on the direct experiences and opinions of students in the class — for example, what personal objects we might take if forced to leave our homes in a hurry, or what memories we have of visiting or moving to a new country. The understanding that the testimonies in this book have been translated into English also provides scope for language awareness work on Arabic and the languages of Africa.

This book can also help to show the realities of problems faced by people in one part of the African continent in a way that avoids underlining negative notions of helplessness in the face of adversity. This is achieved through the quality of the firsthand testimony — presented at young people's own level of awareness — contained inside the pages of *One day we had to run!*

Schools with refugee children

Refugee children may have experienced some of the horrific events described in this book. They may be unwilling to talk about their past as it might jeopardize the safety of family left at home, or because they do not want to feel embarrassed about the popular images of their countries.

However there are ways to make refugee children feel secure while at the same time increasing others' knowledge about their home country. One way may be to mount displays about life in a refugee child's country of origin. Parents and members of refugee community groups could also be invited into the school to tell folk stories and speak to students.

Further resources

Books

Graff, Nancy P. *Where the River Runs: A Portrait of a Refugee Family.* Boston: Little, Brown & Co., 1993.

I Dream of Peace: Images of War by Children of Former Yugoslavia. New York: HarperCollins, 1994.

McCullough, Dennis J. *Kids Coping with War: How Young People React to Military Conflict.* Warren, OH: Alegra House Pubs, 1991.

Ricciuti, Edward R. *Somalia: A Crisis of Famine and War.* Brookfield, CT: Millbrook Press, 1993.

Stewart, Gail B. *Ethiopia.* New York: Macmillan, 1991.

Organizations

American Refugee Committee
2344 Nicollet Avenue South
Suite 350
Minneapolis, MN 55404
Tel: (612) 872-7060

Catholic Relief Services
209 W. Fayette St.
Baltimore, MD 21201
Tel: (410) 625-2220

Children's Aid International
6720 Melrose Ave.
P.O. Box 480155
Los Angeles, CA 90048
Tel: (213) 519-8923
(800) 842-2810 outside CA

Church World Service
Immigration and Refugee Program
475 Riverside Drive; Room 656
New York, NY 10115
Tel: (212) 870-3153

Ethiopian Community Development Council
1036 South Highland St.
Arlington, VA 22204
Tel: (703) 685-0510

International Rescue Committee
386 Park Ave. S.; 10th Fl.
New York, NY 10016
Tel: (212) 679-0100

Save the Children Federation
54 Wilton Rd.
Westport, CT 06880
Tel: (203) 221-4000

U.S. Committee for the United Nations Children's Fund
333 E. 38th Street
New York, NY 10016
Tel: (212) 686-5522

Index

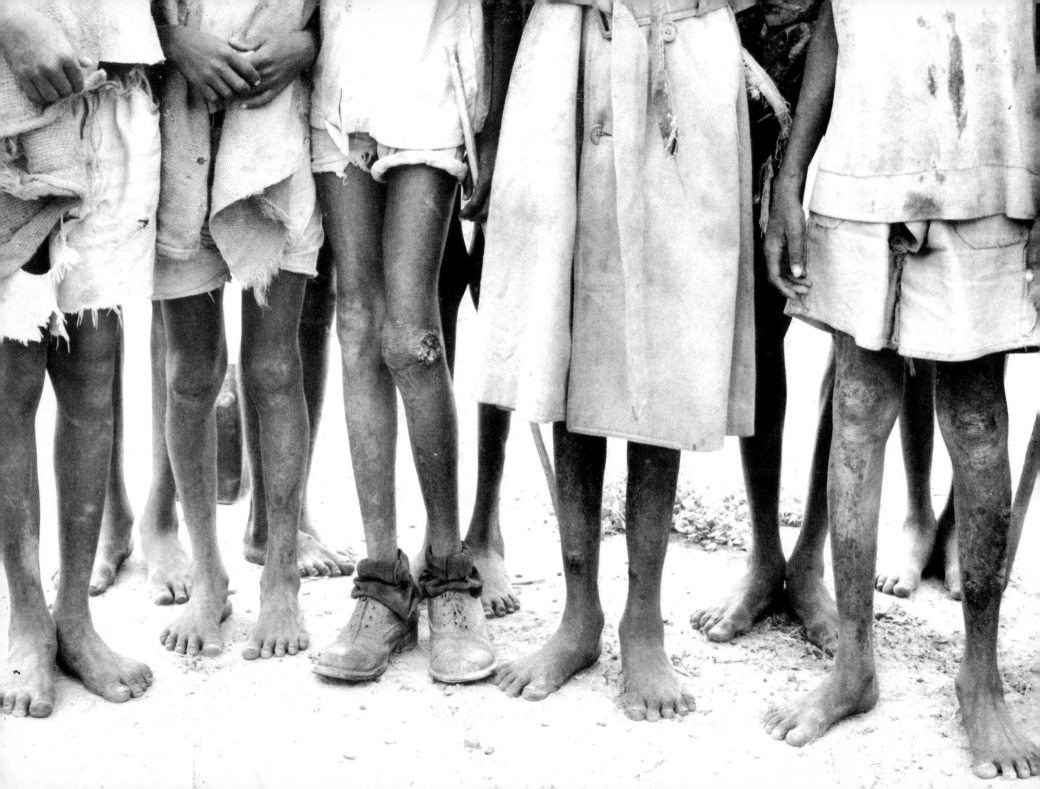